WARNING

Willy 'N Ethel

Turnbull & Willoughby Publishers

WARNING

Willy 'N Ethel

Joe Martin

First printing August, 1984

10 9 8 7 6 5 4 3 2 1

Manufactured in the United States of America

Published by Turnbull & Willoughby Publishers, Inc.
1151 W. Webster, Chicago, Illinois 60614

ISBN: 0-943084-15-6

Bill Dillard, Cover Design

When I was a young man, I inherited a million dollars. I ripped it to shreds and burned it. I then went to the top of a mountain where for the next 10 years, I pondered the mistakes of mankind. One in particular.

Joe Martin

"THEY TURNED ME DOWN BECAUSE I COULDN'T SPELL 'SOAP'... WHAT IS IT, ANYWAYS ?! "

"THIS IS JUAN CARLOS MANUEL PABLO RICARDO AND FOUR OF HIS FRIENDS"

"HERE COMES THAT CLEVER MISTER COB"

"UH OH!. HERE COMES ANOTHER LAWSUIT!"

"I WAS AFRAID YOU'D BE SURPRISED"

"YOU'LL NEVER GUESS WHAT THIS PLACE USED TO BE"

11-15

"WOULD YOU LIKE TO KNOW HOW MUCH MONEY WE'D HAVE
IF I HAD A NICKEL FOR EVERY MINUTE I'VE WASTED?"

SHE'LL
NEVER FIND
ME IN
HERE

11-17

"WELL, ETHEL, HOW'S IT FEEL TO OWN THE WORLD'S LARGEST COLLECTION OF EAGLE-BEAK-TOASTER-LAMP HATS?"

"LET'S LEAVE IT AS IT IS AND CALL IT A 'TYRANNOSAURUS HOOPERDOO'"

"FLOYD HASN'T ADAPTED WELL TO RETIREMENT... I'M SORRY WE EVER SOLD THE STATION"

"OH, LEAVE HIM PLAY WHILE HE'S QUIET"

"NOT BEING STUDENTS OF BODY LANGUAGE, YOU BOYS PROBABLY THINK SHE'S HERE TO GET OUR BEER ORDER"

"HERE COMES THE ONE WITH THE 'BALL-PARK' FIGURES"

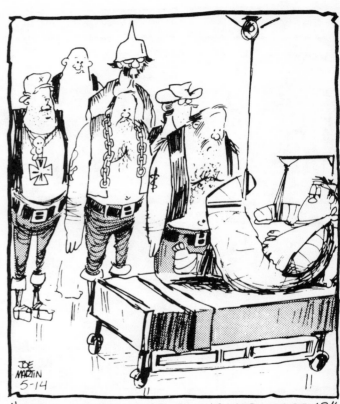

"WOULD IT HELP IF I TOLD YOU WE WERE SORRY?"

"WHADDYA MEAN 'HOW AM I DOING'? HOW'S IT LOOK LIKE I'M DOING!?"

"ARE WE THERE YET?"

"IT'S A SHAME YOU CAN'T SEE WHAT HE'S DOING, HE'S REALLY QUITE GOOD"

"THE COFFEE'S NOT REAL GOOD HERE"

"IT'S OK .. I'M WATCHING HIM"

"WE COULD'VE BEEN REALLY BIG BY NOW IF SCREWBALL OVER THERE WASN'T SO STUBBORN ABOUT WASHING HIS HANDS"

"THERE IT IS, BABE ... THE MARKETER'S DREAM....
THE 'EDDIE SMURPHY' "

"IT'S TIME YOU KNEW, BOY... POLLY AND I AREN'T YOUR REAL PARROTS... YOUR REAL PARROTS DISAPPEARED RIGHT AFTER YOU WERE BORN"

"JUST AS I THOUGHT!... FILLED WITH TINY LITTLE CREDIT COLLECTORS!"

"COULD I GET IN AHEAD OF YOU?"

"I SAY WE HIRE HIM.. IT'D BE WORTH IT JUST TO SEE THE LOOK ON BARNSTORM'S FACE"

"LOOK, I'M TIRED, YOU'RE TIRED.. WE'VE BOTH HAD A LONG DAY.... CAN WE PRETEND I'VE ALREADY GONE BACK AND TALKED TO THE MANAGER?"

"HIS LIFE SAVINGS IS FIFTY CENTS.... THAT'S JUST WALKING-AROUND MONEY FOR ME AND YOU"

"YES.. BUT HAD IT GONE THE OTHER WAY, IT WOULD'VE BEEN ONE OF THE GREATEST FEATS IN SURGICAL HISTORY"

"THE CHEF'S GOING THROUGH SOME SERIOUS PERSONAL PROBLEMS RIGHT NOW AND WE'RE TRYING TO BE AS SUPPORTIVE AS POSSIBLE"

"'LAZY MAN'S WAY TO MAKE A MILLION'!! ETHEL, THIS IS JUST WHAT I'VE BEEN LOOKING FOR!! READ IT TO ME, WILL YA?!"

"BEATS ME HOW A GUY CAN MAKE A LIVING SELLING ONE WORM AT A TIME"

"I BELIEVE YOU'VE MADE A MISTAKE IN OUR ACCOUNT...
ACTUALLY MY HUSBAND WAS THE FIRST TO NOTICE"

"MAYBE YOU SHOULD TRY THE ONE
WITH THE CLOWN ON IT"

"C'MON, ETHEL, IT'S NINETY DEGREES!...
LET SOMEONE ELSE LOOK FOR THE MUSTARD!!"

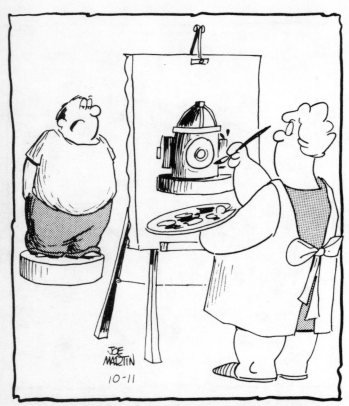

"THIS BETTER NOT BE ANOTHER FIRE HYDRANT"

"HEY, WILLY, GET A LOAD O' THE NUT RUNNIN' DOWN THE HILL WITH THE BOARDS ON HIS FEET!"

" OH, C'MON, IT CAN'T BE THAT BAD! "

5-19

ALL YOU CAN EAT $3.00

"WELL, WE TOOK A CHANCE...WE GAMBLED...AND WE LOST!"

" WELL, ETHEL, DO YOU STILL THINK I'M CRAZY ? "

" THEY'VE ALWAYS BEEN A VERY COMPETITIVE COUPLE "

"FILL THIS BAG WITH MONEY... THEN TAKE OUT A THOUSAND AND GIVE ME THE THERMAL ELECTRIC BLANKET"

"HEY! THAT WAS CLOSE!"

" I GAVE UP TRYIN' TO BE CLEVER SO I FIGURED
I'D JUST NAME IT AFTER YOUR SISTER "

"CLEVER, ETHEL, VERY CLEVER, BUT NOT
CLEVER ENOUGH!"

"WOULD YOU MIND CLOSING THE WINDOW, I'M RUNNING LOW ON NOVOCAINE"

"YOU CAN'T FOOL ME. THE ONLY REASON YOUR SISTER HAS THESE PINOCCHIO PARTIES IS BECAUSE SHE'S TOO CHEAP TO BUY A COSTUME"

"ETHEL, QUICK, BEHIND YOU!!
OPEN YOUR MOUTH!!"

"HMM.. A NOTE.. I WONDER WHAT IT SAYS...?
THAT'S ODD... AN ECHO."

"I MEAN, WHAT DO YOU CALL IT ASIDE FROM YOURS!?"

" THEY'RE GAINING ON US "

"IT'S FROM READER'S DIGEST, WE'RE THE FIRST ONES THEY'VE ELIMINATED"

8-31

"I'D HATE TO BE THE ONE THAT STOLE HIS SKIS"

12-11

"THERE I WAS AT THE **TEN**!.. THE **TWENTY**!.. THE ONE THAT COMES AFTER THAT!.. THE ONE THAT COMES AFTER THAT!.."

"HE THROWS THE STICKS IN THE AIR, I WAVE THE BAGS,... IT'S ALL SO MEANINGLESS"

"C'MON, ETHEL! STOP KIDDIN' AROUND, GIMME THE ANTIDOTE!"

"C'MON IN AND EAT. YOU CAN FINISH UP AFTER DINNER"

"I SEE YOU'VE MET EVERYONE"

5-12

DR. Z. B. FELZNIC
ACUPUNCTURE

10-5

"I REALLY SHOULD SERVE ALL 3 MEALS AT THE SAME TIME.. IT'S SILLY FOR YOU TO BE JUMPING UP AND DOWN LIKE THIS EVERY FOUR HOURS"

"SOMEBODY MUST'VE MADE A MISTAKE... HOW CAN THESE BE THE CHEAP SEATS ?!"

"SHE'S GOT 'EM ALL OVER TOWN ...I CAN'T MAKE A MOVE"

12-5

"HI, HON, I'M HOME"

11-29

"IS THAT AS FAR AS YOU CAN THROW ?! "

"HALF OF ME SAID 'DUCK,' BUT THE OTHER HALF SAID 'WHAT IF IT'S BLUEBERRY ?' "

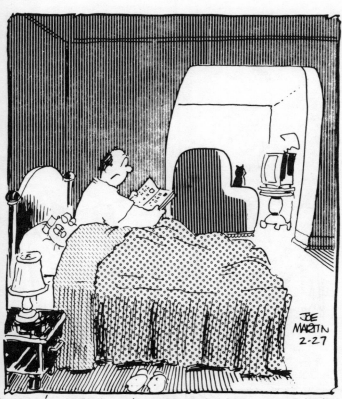

THERE'S NOTHING ON.. NOTHING AT ALL... JUST JUNK!
THAT CAT'S NUTS!! "

" VITO... WANNA GET ME A PRICE ON PEACH PITS ? "

"LISTEN, IF IT'LL CHEER YOU UP ANY YOU CAN SIT UP HERE AND BE CAPTAIN FOR A WHILE"

"SAY, IS THIS BY ANY CHANCE THE GREAT-GRANDDADDY OF THAT GREEN AND BLUE THING IN THE BACK OF THE REFRIGERATOR?"

"HERE HE COMES, TURN AROUND!"

HEY.. I JUST BROKE A TOOTH ON ONE OF THESE MEATBALLS!

3-23

"GUY WANTS TO KNOW HOW MUCH 'AMBIANCE' THEY PUT IN THIS STUFF... 'BOUT A QUART, RIGHT?!"

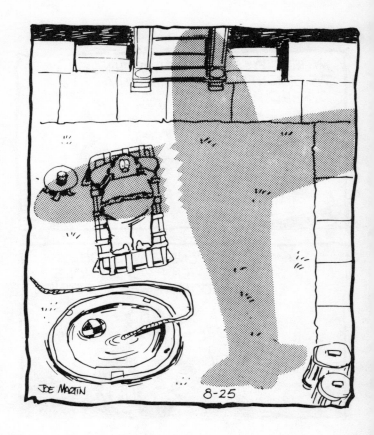

8-25

"OK ..WHAT'S BUGGIN' YOU ?.. A GUY CAN'T BE MARRIED TO A GIRL FOR 15 YEARS AND NOT KNOW WHEN SOMETHING'S UP."

"I DON'T MEAN TO COMPLAIN, DEAR... BUT ISN'T THIS WATER A LITTLE SOUPY?"

"I COULDN'T GET IT OUT SO I MADE IT LOOK LIKE AN ALLIGATOR"

"I KNOW THIS IS PROBABLY GOING TO UPSET YOUR PLANS, BUT SOMETHING'S COME UP, AND MY SISTER AND HER HUSBAND CAN'T MAKE IT TONIGHT"

6-10

"BOY, I HAVEN'T WORN A TIE IN SUCH A LONG TIME I CAN'T EVEN REMEMBER WHICH POCKET YOU'RE SUPPOSED TO TUCK IT INTO"

9/14   JEMARTIN

"LET'S GET A HARDCOVER BOOK AND FIX
THE THING PERMANENTLY! ONCE AND FOR ALL!"

"THIS IS MY HUSBAND, GEORGE, OUR SON, GEORGE II AND OUR NEWEST ADDITION 'RETURN TO THE PLANET OF GEORGE'"

"CUP YOUR HAND, CUP YOUR HAND!"

"I'M GONNA MEASURE YOUR WAIST..NOW
HOLD THE TAPE HERE AND IF I'M NOT
BACK BY DAWN CALL THE SHERIFF"

"ALL I CAN SAY IS WHOEVER TOLD YOU TWO NOT
TO PANIC MUST'VE BEEN OUT OF THEIR MIND"

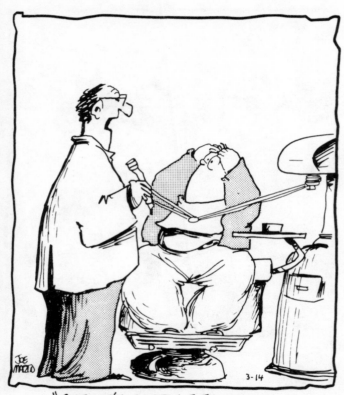

"GEEZ, I'M SORRY, I THOUGHT
YOU WERE TALLER"

"WHAT A STUPID GAME !"

7-18

"I BET I CAN MAKE YOU TALK LIKE AN INDIAN "

6-29

LISTEN, ETHEL, IF WE'RE GOING TO HANDLE THIS LIKE MATURE ADULTS, I'M GONNA NEED MORE TIME TO BUILD MY FORT!

"YOUR NEPHEW TOOK YOUR CAMERA APART, CLEANED THE LENSES, ADJUSTED THE SHUTTERS, REALIGNED THE GEARS, AND NOW IT'S A PAPERWEIGHT"

"FROM NOW ON, FINNEGAN, LET THE BALD-HEADED PEOPLE SIT WHEREVER THEY WANT!"

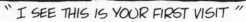
"I SEE THIS IS YOUR FIRST VISIT"

"THE WORST THING ABOUT THIS IS WHEN I GET HOME I'M GONNA HAVE TO LISTEN TO THE OL' 'SO YOU GOT YOUR HEAD STUCK IN A BUCKET AGAIN' LECTURE FOR ABOUT THE 13 ZILLIONTH TIME"

"GO AHEAD, GO AHEAD, I'M LISTENING"

"LOOK, IT'S YOUR DECISION.. DO YOU WANT STYLE OR DO YOU WANT TO BE AERODYNAMICALLY SOUND?"

"NOW YOU'RE SURE YOU HAVEN'T BEEN STICKING YOUR THUMB IN YOUR MOUTH AND BLOWING ON IT?"

"WELL, WELL, WELL... THE OL' BALLOON-
COVERED-WITH-GRAVY' TRICK "

"WELL THEN, HOW ABOUT CARDBOARD? DO YOU
LOVE ME MORE THAN CARDBOARD ?! "

"LET ME PUT IT TO YOU THIS WAY... IF WE WERE PIONEERS THIS IS WHERE WE'D BUILD THE CABIN"

"HEAR THAT, JOHNSON? I'M IN MY POOL AGAIN!... EAT YOUR HEART OUT!"

"LOOKS LIKE MRS. HOWARD'S INADVERTENTLY PUT ANOTHER HAM IN HER COAT"

4-27

"WELL, WELL, WELL, WELL, WELL... AND WHAT DO WE HAVE HERE ?! "

" ETHEL, WHERE'S YOUR MANNERS ? AREN'T YOU GOING TO OFFER RALPH A BEER FOR THE RIDE HOME ?"

"IF I'D STUDIED, GONE TO COLLEGE, WORKED HARDER AND MADE SOMETHING OF MYSELF, I COULD PROBABLY FIGURE OUT A BETTER WAY TO DO THIS"

Jal's TRICKS + NOVELTIES

BANG

"WELL, FOLKS, WHAT'S IT GONNA BE, THE WHOOPEE COSHION, THE PHONY SOAP OR THE SPIKE BINOCULARS?"

JOE MARTIN

"ISN'T THIS THE SAME WAY 'JAWS I' ENDED?"